D1467185

BNP

OTHER EDITIONS IN THIS SERIES

George Garrett, guest editor, *Best New Poets 2005*

Eric Pankey, guest editor, *Best New Poets 2006*

Natasha Tretheway, guest editor, *Best New Poets 2007*

Mark Strand, guest editor, *Best New Poets 2008*

Kim Addonizio guest editor, *Best New Poets 2009*

Claudia Emerson, guest editor, *Best New Poets 2010*

D.A. Powell, guest editor, *Best New Poets 2011*

Matthew Dickman, guest editor, *Best New Poets 2012*

Brenda Shaughnessy, guest editor, *Best New Poets 2013*

Dorianne Laux, guest editor, *Best New Poets 2014*

Tracy K. Smith, guest editor, *Best New Poets 2015*

Best
NEW
Poets

2016

50 Poems from Emerging Writers

Guest Editor Mary Szybist

Series Editors Jeb Livingood and Angie Hogan

This book was published in cooperation with *Meridian* (readmeridian.org) and the University of Virginia Press (upress.virginia.edu).

For additional information, visit us at
bestnewpoets.org
twitter.com/BestNewPoets
facebook.com/BestNewPoets

Cover and interior design elements by Atomicdust | atomicdust.com

Text set in Adobe Garamond Pro and Bodini

Printed by Bailey Printing, Charlottesville, Virginia

ISBN: 978-0-9975623-0-9
ISSN: 1554-7019

Contents

About *Best New Poets*

Welcome to *Best New Poets 2016*, our twelfth installment of fifty poems from emerging writers. In *Best New Poets*, the term "emerging writer" is defined as someone who has yet to publish a book-length collection of poetry. The goal of *Best New Poets* is to provide special encouragement and recognition to new poets, the many writing programs they attend, and the magazines that publish their work.

From February to May of 2016, *Best New Poets* accepted nominations from writing programs and magazines in the United States and Canada. Each magazine and program could nominate two writers, each of whom could send a free submission to the anthology for consideration. For a small reading fee, writers who had not received nominations could submit poems as part of our open competition. Eligible poems were either published after January 1, 2015, or unpublished.

In all, we received over 2,100 submissions for a total of roughly 4,050 poems. A pool of readers and the series editors ranked these submissions, sending a few hundred selections to this year's guest editor, Mary Szybist, who chose the final fifty poems.

The series editors wish to thank our readers,

Kate Coleman, Caitlin Fitzpatrick, Courtney Flerlage, Landis Grenville, Caitlin Neely, Annie Pittman, and Rob Shapiro.

We also want to thank Jason Coleman, Jazzy Danziger, and Atomicdust for their editorial advice and support.

Mary Szybist wishes to thank Sara Guest for her friendship and wise counsel during the course of this project.

Charif Shanahan

Song

I wait each night for a self.
I say *the mist*, I say *the strange*
tumble of leaves, I say *a motor*
in the distance, but I mean
a self and *a self* and *a self.*
A small cold wind
coils and uncoils in the corner
of every room. A vagrant.
In the dream
I gather my life in bundles
and stand at the edge of a field
of snow. It is a field I know
but have never seen. It is
nowhere and always new:
What about the lives
I might have lived?
As who? And who
will be accountable
for this regret I see
no way to avoid? A core,
or a husk, I need to learn
not how to speak, but *from where.*
Do you understand? I say
name, but I mean *a conduit*
from me to me, I mean *a net*,
I mean *an awning of stars.*

Max McDonough
Makeshift Bildungsroman

My mother—blogger, doll addict,
cyber queen, sniper
at the eBay auction computer screen—

had the tendency to mix her idioms.
From the get-go, for example,
became *from the gecko*

when she said it. *Not the sharpest
bowling ball in the shed.
He side-blinded me. Shithead thinks he's cool*

as mustard. Thinks he's right up my sleeve.
I escaped from New Jersey
for college, which *opened up a whole nother*

can of germs. In emails I wrote: *Professor,
I'll have to mow it over a little longer.
Professor, without a question of a doubt.*

I didn't realize I made switches too
until I re-read them—a nervous,
first-gen scholarship student—

as I'm sure my mother didn't think
she'd altered anything
in her life. But that's a different chiasmus

for a different line of thought,
not for nights like this one, alone
and happy mostly, my heart *at the peck and call,*

though, of those suburban woods
of my childhood again—
the ultraviolet yellow feathers

of witch-hazel thicket, serrated
huckleberry leaves—the understory
so dense, tangled to itself, that walking

a straight line becomes
a tight circle, and my mother's voice is mine.

Joy Priest
Ode to Hushpuppy

say *here* & it sound
like a heel   shoved

down a throat,
a horse hitched,   guttural.

tough meat yanked,
bones crushed by   teeth

minted in gold. sound
like a sixth   generation

curse when it fly
out your mouth   little god.

a bolt cracking 'cross
field laid flat beneath   indigo

clouds. you say *come back*
heel & you   mean

your daddy too, mean
we are so   ancient.

how long we done
lived—   us-folk,

for whom heaven
is a live   broadcast

everyone else gets
to simply   watch.

our down-at-the-heel
place, filthy &   barefoot,

double-wide on stilts,
a body to be   burned

if need be, 'cause
already. already no   fear

of fire in you
of sharp gill or a   heavy

hand laid into your cheek.
you've   caught

on early, turning—
through the   cylinders

of nature—root,
rainfall to praise.   making

rubber tire, rusted
scrap into   playground.

sun-bleached boats,
fish nets are   birds

in your hand,
there on the divine   screen

of poverty. ingenuity,
beggar's   alchemy:

what we got into
what we ain't   meant

to have. *we's*
who the   *earth*

is for, you
squeak &   you sing

two kinds of people:
your daddy &   you:

those who stay
& those who   survive

but won't ever escape
the down   heel.

Wren Hanks
The Ghost Incites a Genderqueer Pledge of Allegiance

Deny *girl* and the blood galaxies trailing it; there is a ghost in me who loves each egg, who won't let me throw up when I'm seasick from my period.

There is a ghost in me riffing on fertility & chocolate almonds. *We grow organs in pig ribs, ghost.* Surely swelling and blossoming are not the same.

Swelling's for an injured brain, a uterus drunk on the repetition of cells. I place my hand on my bound chest, pledge allegiance to the rashes and the scales, the fold and petal.

It's a mess inside me, ghost.

Sam Cha
Word Problem: Heart

If you are nine and your heart is a heart an American heart like lately mine. If you are nine if you're a girl if you're a girl named Aiyana if you have a dad if you love your dad. If your dad is an American man a black man. If your dad who gave you your eyes your cheekbones your chin your grin. If your dad hugged you one night extra tight one night when you were five and there were tears in his eyes, if you were scared you didn't know dads could cry. If when you heard your dad and your mom talking about Aiyana, Aiyana *shot by a cop*, you thought they were talking about you, *poor little girl*, and you were scared. If they said *just a baby, only seven years old, Aiyana Jones.* If you were angry then, *why are they scaring me like that, some girl who doesn't have anything to do with me, some other little girl.* If when you turned seven you felt bad all day you couldn't keep worry out of your head, cloudy and nothing tasted as sweet as it looked, and your mom asking *Aiyana what's wrong baby* and you saying *nothing momma I don't know my belly hurts leave me alone*, and the whole time you were waiting to be dead. If you didn't die. If you are nine now you are big, not as big as your sister who is ten but you are big you are bigger than your little sister who is one. If you are hungry one night *daddy can I have something to eat* so your dad goes out to get you some food your dad goes to get you some burgers. If you're hungry, and *he's taking so long and what is he doing, why is it taking him so long.* If you are angry *didn't I tell daddy I was so hungry so hungry belly inside out like an old shirt.* If the phone rings then. If your mom answers. If she starts to scream. If later you write a letter, a letter to the cop who shot your father, the white man who shot your dad your daddy your father your arms around you, your *carry me daddy,* your *I left my bear in the living room daddy,* your *daddy can i have some milk,* your *daddy good night,* your *daddy look at this,* your *I love you daddy,* your *daddy can I have a hug,* your *daddy don't go.* If you are nine and your heart is an American heart and it hurts and you go to the paper you pick up a pencil and you begin to write and you hurt your heart hurts and when you write you write *to the officer that killed my dad let me tell you something you heart three little girls that look up to their dad.* If your heart hearts. If you're all heart. If it hearts, it hearts so much. Then, America. What is a heart? Why do we keep it going, beating heart into heart into heart?

Elizabeth O'Brien
At the Academy for Muses

They could all be teenagers. They vamp and pout, or so we imagine
they drape, swanning back all wingspan, all broody eyes long-lashed,
almond roasted, liquid lines. They study the history of movement,

the art of plumbing limbs down arms of chaises, atop feather-ticks
or oh, any old stained-from-the-yard mattress will do. They turn
slumps to fawns, to gazelles and everyone has a neck like a willow

branch or a violin, a neck drenched in satin and light
fingers scrolling as grace notes for hands. They take extra
credits in Disaffection, failing to see humor in this, and

if their eyes are dead or tormented by some unnamable thing,
we'd offer it up in exchange for their dewy brow lines,
their stung lips deliriously bitten, plump as the moist flesh

of a plum or the feel of a word like *each. Each lip.* Do they
practice on words? Like *luminous*, like *lily*, like *endive*.
Do they practice being cookbook photography, or tattoos

fresh-inked so slick so every every want bumps up the skin
to a raised line of gasp? To be pushed down just *so*
with the thumb: faded or bleached or pricked pin-fine

with holes or the nipple hinting everywhere or the freckle,
each freckle freckle we want to put our fingers here where
light itself is rich as olives and as musky-sweet. Look, now

they shear a single red-skinned apple on a blade
between poses, like mica each cleaved sheet goes
honey-tart on a pointed tongue. They infer angles, light

hits and shadows knee bones, quartering out
the convex of a stomach, a hip.
Musing is a practice of rumpled

hair, parted lips, asymmetry. Desire
and inspiration aren't lovers, really
but trick mirrors, smoked glass.

Anders Carlson-Wee
To the Fingerless Man in Banff

There was little you couldn't do.
With the purple stump of your thumb
you pinned a pencil against
the knuckle-lumps, forming enough grip
to sketch her portrait from memory,
or from the photo you kept hid
in your hatband. You worked the ranches
like before. Rode horses. Knotted
ropes. Shuffled when you dealt.
You let me ball old newsprint
for the fire, but you did everything else.
Gutted the fish. Stuffed the belly
with berries and butter and smoked it
by rotating a willow stick.
And when you folded your hands
to whisper the words over the meal,
nothing folded, but what kind of world
would this be if that mattered?
Your cheeks filled and flickered
as you chewed. The embers bedded down
and the clouds born out of them
twisted through the cottonwoods.
You never told me her name.
That could jinx it, you said.
*If I find her again it ain't gonna be
as a detective.* You could even roll
your own cigarettes, but you couldn't
roll the striker on a Bic.

I flicked it alive for you. Your palms
pulled my hand toward your lips.

Will Cordeiro
Open Country

You scan the foothills where an outline shifts:
each vaster distance gives a clearer view
within—each vista where you look and look,
and every figure is transformed to nothing
but shadows walking at the edge of dusk.

Then past some cloverleaf, a Motel 6
shines then dims, its ice machine still laughing
to itself. A vacant moon tricks out the clouds
over fields like gold we have no standards for,
far jack pines sopping up the last dark light.

Ride on. A scarecrow gnawed to sticks and rags;
a hide left curing next to guts its spilled,
which tortured flies have claimed by squatter's rights.
One day your heart will rot like gopherwood.
You'll wake and watch a river pour away.

Jody Rambo

Elegy in Which My Mother Learns to Swim

There appears a tree, and next to it a horse, still and unsaddled
and she is saying something of comfort to it
by way of touch. In warmth of bone the moonlight steadies
on a small lake, the one in which as a child she
washed her sister's hair. She leads the horse obliging, through thicket
and sawgrass rough against her shins, to the water
having the look of dark risk and a little loneliness.
She cannot take her eyes away from the blackest leg of the horse
bending to paw the water. Nor the milklight
of her own skin dipping beneath the surface. Nothing so dark
as a lake bottom, so blind as branches from their
high lookout above her—the imperfect swimmer—whose history
is dry land, a shoreline of nervous wings. Cling
she does, with her arms around the muscular belly of the horse
who will teach her the word *deep,* ground her to water
which will be her release. And into the lash of its watery mane
she will speak the real names of the world, transcribed
on her tongue to the taste of rain. Swift passenger now. No longer
mother of fearful disposition, riding herself bareback
into the darkness of her childhood and out again,
loosed from the being of a body, a soul become a stitchery
of wild grass, of leaf and sky—she rides free. And the horse
belonging to no one, finding her warm against its back,
feels her breath in a new dominion of wind, and follows
the nudge of her legs ahold a horizon, its thin swayback of love.
Had I only known this night coming, I would have learned
to be as still as lake water around her, to offer my hand—as a bidding,
like a burning, a quench, a touch I longed for, undaughtered
on this day I call morning, call loving her however I can.

Caitlin Scarano
Mule

Father's coffin and the petals
of an opening mouth.
He was an absence,
a complete absorption of light.

Tongue's rot, funeral rot—
these are not the same.

Master made by hound. Man
and the dog he drags
by an invisible length of rope.
Shepherd, give me back
my country of winter.
Give me back silence

between bleached streets. Moon
resting her belly on the tin roof
of a farmhouse. Mother hiding
sounds of sobbing behind a marble
handled door. The creatures of her own

father's hands. The warm eggs
I found between the bricks
near the coop, how sometimes
the harder surfaces are where
we need to nest.

Mule I made from pillow innards,
chicken wire, and the leather
of a lampshade. The difference
between infertility and impotency.

We all had a choice.

I set fire to the Virginia field and rode
out. Made for a mountain, her
crown of snow. A single
spider crossed my cheek.

How I untangled
the fishing wire from flesh.
How I learned to unlove that man
before I swallowed the hook
of his death.

Nandini Dhar
A Brief History of Clamor

Like a cabinet, a goddess is crafted: like this city whittling its own little girls. Satin the color of car fumes, pleats abrasive against the hair in our armpits, elbows and knees. A bruise on the shiuli petal stuck in the mud, its orange stem upturned, the imprints of a car tire on the knee-caps of my sister. There is a poem hidden inside this lump of clay, in hands that bend silt into immaculately chiseled cheeks. We do have a word reserved for potters who formulate loam into divine. What we do not have is a word for little girls who want to store that knowledge in discarded matchboxes.

In the raven's beak, this knowledge, absconding. In the fingers of every artisan, memoirs of necessary defilements, how the mundane is indented on the faces of the goddesses we make. A starlet rode by her bike yesterday: past the dried canal, the carcasses of the cars, the abandoned factory gates. There was no reason for us to know this. But her wheels got stuck in the razor-thin cracks of the cobblestones. Her ghagra flowing like the petals of hibiscus: purple silk, intricate thread birds. Alabaster face, gossamer arms. Every one of us memorized her, bit by bit. A little at a time. And she vanished. Vanished under the pressure of our eyelids, became the steam in our grandmother's teacup.

Where she vanished, we don't know. And don't want to know. But our goddesses are to be schooled. Schooled in stamping a face on clay, to impress on divinity what is mortal. This is also how we ghost our goddesses, insert our own fingers in the distance between the dead and the divine, make dolls of their clay limbs. Last year, it happened to be the dead queen from a far-off land. This year, the vanished actress. In the courtyard, my sister is skinning sparrows. She is done with nineteen of them: eighty-nine remain to be peeled. Drums are to be fashioned out of dead sparrow skin. A step forward in schooling the goddesses we worship: how and when to make space for the demons they kill as ritual marks. *Beauty is nothing but the shadow of a blood drop on a needle tip*, says the neighborhood madman. A blur, a sound, a rhythm: *do or die.*

Do. Do. Do. Die. Die. Die. The taste of ash on my tongue, fire in between their teeth. Our littlest uncles, no blood relatives to us, are dancing. Dancing to repossess the dead. Broken twigs, polythene bags, newspaper shards whirling about, my sister, thick as a myth, is letting loose her banyan root hair. She swallows an owl, and does not even burp. I am scared of nor'westers and sister shouts. Shouts an order: *quit painting those damn toadstools blue.* A day ago, our grandmother threw away a bowlful of Maggi noodles, thinking they were overgrown maggots. Wrapping them on her fingers like threads. One by one. We are learning. Learning to wrest our tongues on what is slippery. Sister has just begun to let the crow's nest inside her curls. While skinning sparrows.

Me, Toi, on my way to a hidden closure—fishhooked inside a rosewood box, a hyacinth purple skirt to twirl. Here, in the middle of our courtyard, a face is what my sister sculpts for me—a sharp half-moon, scythe-shaped. Like obsolete poems. I watch through the keyhole. Dust in her hair, dust on her tongue, hands spread. My sister is dancing. Dancing with our uncles, the summer storm between her fingertips. She is chewing its brown feathers alive. It was our birthday yesterday, and in the pages of her notebook, new resolutions: *a book a day keeps everyone away. Make the rail station as much of a home as these rooms.* But what is more, sister has resolved never to turn twelve.

A new ritual mark: this is how fair-skinned goddesses learn make space for demons they had once been taught to kill. My sister is learning to befriend whatever the goddesses were meant to kill— a darkness that resembles the raven's feathers, a blue that echoes the starlit sky. This is how this city whittles its own little girls, and we let her.

Ariel Francisco
Meditation on Patience

Of patience, I know only
what sea turtles have taught me:
how they are born on lightless
beaches so the moon can serve
as a beacon to lure them
into the water; how they spend
their whole lives trying to swim
towards it, enamored, obsessed;
how they flap their forelimbs,
a vague recollection of flying—
the right movement in the wrong
medium, as if they knew how
to reach the moon in a former life
but now only remember the useless
persistent motions; how if you cut
one's heart out it would keep
beating in the pit of your palm,
recognizing the cold night air.

Jenny Boychuk
Apeirophobia

—fear of infinity
with thanks to Jamaal May

—because what is linear or non-linear
cannot explain why the first arrow

Artemis pulled back between two fingers
punctured no beast's skin, drew no

blood—but floated, flickering on & on
through a forest of pine & cedar. An eternal

miss: spring disappeared again & again.
Foxgloves withdrew into their tombs

of root. Did Apollo whisper to his sister
in the womb? Are they whispering now

in the blue shade of a garden? Blooming
& re-blooming—bent-over, orchid-spined,

my brother & I climbed a trail choked
with vines, up the last volcano, mud coating

our calves. At the top we swung our legs
over the edge, but could not see the end

of its hot throat. No longer dormant inside,
the beast snapped open its eyes: not a fear

of death, but the fleeting idea of being
re-born to a mother who instinctively

knows to dress us in black—

Julian Gewirtz
The Gang's All Here

> "Nature's Grand Hotel has its Season, like the others. As the
> guests one by one pack, pay, and depart, and the seats at the
> *table-d'hôte* shrink pitifully at each succeeding meal....Why not
> stay on quietly here, like us, and be jolly?"
> —Kenneth Grahame, *The Wind in the Willows*

Don't sit too close, the smell
of her perfume is somehow
here still on this mondegreen
cableknit, I'm wearing it anyway

because you'd like that,
if I reminded you of her,
you'd never say. She checks out
of the Grand Hotel Nature

with the lean vacationers
all still sunning
on the whitening dock,
those boys whose shoulders

grow wider with each meal
and girls whose voices ring
more of birdsong
than half the birds here,

loud mallards buoying
the hazards of that black
water, heads gleaming
with richest green velvet

like the chair she climbs
kicked away.
But you know that part
of the story, you find her there

a pendulum stilled.
Meantime I in the marble bar
pressed against what
experts name *serpentine*,

dark green stone-scales
which Romans thought
to resemble a coiled whip-
snake that could not bite.

Jen Jabaily-Blackburn
Braintree

All of this was farmland once. When they came to
build the incinerator, my father dressed like a
masked outlaw. His friends carried six-foot pencils.
My sister and I carried Mike Dukakis in a tank. Our
mother carried us children home, and the adults had
sandwiches in jail. All of this is true. Jellyfish found
belly-up in the salt marsh. So small as to look
harmless. When possible, our passions are graspable.
Mandatory karaoke Fridays, Jade or Golden Bowl.
Always a choice. One church or the other. All of this
was farmland once. Where we are dancing was once
a horse. Helen, late of the old country, please choose:
dogged fire or glowing grate. Machined lace for
every maple table. Beloved cypress paneling new
owners haul out. Rhotic lack the shibboleth. All of us
are from here, but some are more from here than
others. On the classroom wall, the lonely Yeats
watching over brass-chained glasses down his nose. I
propose we build in Watson Park a shrine to last
working payphones. Stars deceptively near and yet
so small as to look harmless. St. Brigid's friable cross
above the door. Cigarette fires rip the cattails in the
marsh. Glass shards in the parking lot a wrecked
diadem. No country for old Helens. Blonde Mr.
Phys-Ed oils his feet in the center of the library.
Unforgivable. Doughy feet gleaming like combative
seals under the fluorescents. His younger self locked
in the mural in the foyer. The mascot, a bodiless

feathered chief, cast as his fawning moon. The
building's architecture is considered to be Brutalist.
Napthal smell on the tracks off Pond. The last actual
nuns wandering the drugstore. The replica Umbrian
church, terracotta in snow. St. Francis's living
epaulets. Francis, patron saint of animals, though
always the same: small passerines, rabbits, deer. You
never see St. Francis attended by porcupines. You
never see him cradling a jellyfish, its gas flame cool in
his palm. Fore River and ever and ever. Bonus moon
bobbing on the surface, belly-up. Our excuse for the
sea, so small as to look harmless.

Jennie Malboeuf
Grandmothers

Where does it all begin?
God is good; woman bleeds.
It was the depression or before.
You were cooking over an open
greasy fire and the house burned
to the ground. And you were cutting
the heads off chickens and laughing
at the horror of them walking backward
and dancing. And you were slitting
the throats of two-hundred-pound hogs.
And keeping your future husband
from priesthood with seven children.
You showed me my stuffed puppy
legs in the air. *He's dead!* you said.
Or you were a little girl with an iron
and a board for Christmas. You learned
to drive stick in a field. And you gave
birth to father jumping off trains
or you gave birth to mother
who only gave birth to two.
You were a witch, our house
adorned with dead animals,
fish curling to free themselves
from the wall.

Jesse De Angelis
American Spacesuit

for Hazel Fellows

In this room, the Singers are always running
through a man's shape, thread in lockstitch.

Some of us are always here, working.
Julia dips the shells in latex, Velma glues

the layers of Mylar together. Me, I sew.
Today is the part that touches skin,

that lets his own heat warm him.
This needle's the only thing that gets so close.

/

It's a job, no one's dream. Later, I'll see him
on TV, floating naked and warm

inside what I made for him. We never saw
their faces. I read his measurements off a card.

//

We used to make smaller, softer things.
Underwear. We cut, we sewed. We knew

all the shapes a body could be made to take.
There are only some things fabric won't do.

///

That first day we switched what we sewed,
our bosses called us all over. Said

we'd have to learn it all over again,
like a second first time. They took my pins,

doled them back out slow. Just the thinnest layer
between this and nothing.

////

We already knew the rest of it:
how to hold the threads, the way layers lap

over one another. Every way the suit
could fold and hang, where not to follow

the pattern's lines with our scissors. Already,
I knew the ways cloth can keep a body safe.

/////

And if they found a stray pin,
they'd stick it into your skin.

//////

When the suit was all shaped and layered,
when it finally looked like the man I'd imagined

white and headless on the worktable, we sent him off.
He came back wearing a little card

saying where he didn't fit. It took days
to slice apart each stitch, unpiecing

carefully everything we'd made around him.
Then we began it again.

/

The machines had been set to run
too fast through him, needles eating up

the fabric thread by thread. So our treadles changed,
I sewed slower. Each stitch was one footfall.

Yes, he'll fly. But first, I'll walk
the whole way out for him.

//

And what I'm doing is sitting
in a white room in Dover, Delaware.

Hundred of hands are passing his shape
back and forth under the banks of fluorescents.

Mine feed fabric into my machine;
I'm thinking about the easy way

smoke could be rising from a cigarette's lit tip.
How, in rising, it becomes nothing.

Jo Brachman
The Scientist's Hypothesis of Distance

Blue nothing. She considered miles
out the high window in the stairwell.
First, simple paper distances her finger

could trace, point A to point B.
Then more difficult measurement,
that of closeness, like bonded atoms.

And then, hypothetical expanses
like those of the heart's vessels—
their length could circle the globe twice.

A plane seemed to crawl across the glass,
leaving a necklace vapor trail. She believed
in possibilities, that every atom that could exist,

already did, but still, she could not wear the red,
strapless dress she no longer owned,
couldn't lift her hair for his fingertips to clasp

pearls at the nape of her neck, his breath
fastening a shiver between her shoulder blades
down the small dip of her back.

She wanted to look into a large aperture
telescope, to view the farthest reaches
of visible space, where no energy had ever been

destroyed, to see into the incalculable vastness
of him in their living room downstairs, him
on the brown sofa reading. She wanted

him to put down his book, to think of her
on the landing, waiting. For him to move
exponentially faster, up the stairs two at a time.

Erick Piller
Jar

The dirt turns in it as I turn it, soundlessly
though I expected a sound, even a slight one,
the dirt falling along the curve as true
as a compass needle points north, falling
toward ground. As if the dirt could feel
itself in fellowship with the ground
beneath this grass—*of the earth*. It's not
just the strangeness of the discovery
that holds the jar aloof (around it, the brittle, golden
grass, the spongy ground) but the perfection
of it: of its roundness, its dusted transparency,
the words in perfect script across it: "Sweet
Honey Moon." Inside the jar, in the lip
of a curve, there's a fine coating
of dirt that sticks as if caught, like an ant,
in some last trace of honey. But my eye
rests on the chip, like a lower-case *v*,
at the mouth of the jar, like a word about to be
uttered. This could be a kind of apology,
maybe, for its perfection, for being so out
of place in this place of raggedness,
yellowed stems, disgusting squirrels that shine
in their grease and bark from behind tufts of leaves
at me and my dog. Or if not, an apology,
a retraction. A quid pro quo. The jar
took no dominion; it never called
the wilderness to a helpless, circus-like
tameness around it, like a snake

charmer, or like a hypnotist might. It fell—how?—
it was discarded. It filled with rain-
water, then mud, then dirt. Filled with light,
then, when night fell, dark—but now
it was always full, somehow:
with earth, which also contained *it*,
or half of it. It was half buried, brimming
half with earth, half with air. And light
filled that air. And roots, like lightning
frozen beneath the stalks of grass, closed
in around the jar and opened inside it.
No one could say how long it had stayed
this way, because the jar had nearly
vanished into the woods—but the rainwater
had come again and now the jar
was loosened. Not "beautiful,"
not by any traditional measure,
but something that the light could catch
on, as clear and strange in those
woods as I was just then, turning in
my hands a decades-old jar, expecting a sound
from it, even a rain stick's soft sliding,
and being surprised, at that moment,
by the opening movement of a storm.

—Nominated by the University of Connecticut

John James
Poem Around Which Everything Is Structured

On his third night of dreams the boy turning in his bed
      hums about goodness & trees. He sees the berries
in his palm, which are the final berries of the season,

      so he squeezes them to watch their juice bleed through
the dim crevasses of his hand. Something's missing
      in this song & I don't know what it is. A shadow, maybe,

or a light between trees. Tonight, as the stars seep
      through his window & touch the dusty water he keeps
sitting in a glass by his bed, the boy wonders what it would be

      to touch the body of another. I search his eyes
for mutual absence. And maybe as I map the freckles
      on his wrist, as the song crescendos, as the night fades into

dull purples & blues—maybe the lights go out & I feel
      his breath on my hand. Or maybe that's wrong, too.
Maybe I become the delicate prison he attends to, the cold

      thread wending in & out his chest, the rapture he feels
when he dangles me from the wood post of his gallows.
      Suppose I wrote this song in another key entirely.

I could cast it in a way that doesn't care about touching
      & hips. The boy could carry a spade out into the yard
& drop it down into the soil, where the earth would dance

around it & the stars shrink into the distance until they
disappear between hills. This is how I think, Love,
      about you. This is how I structure everything around me

that needs to be structured—the taste buds on your tongue,
      the salt of your wrist, the shape of your mouth as you
tell me every little thing you ever wanted me to know.

      I want to give him a name, that boy. I want to call that name
on nights when the ceiling hangs low above my bed,
      & the plaster cracks, & the sky pokes through the minute

slits between blinds. I want to feel his hands, not my hands,
      shivering in the wool sleeves of my coat, anything
but the same shaking of the leaves, the orchid dying bloom

      by bloom in the window while its naked stem bends
a single blossom toward the sun. It delights in a small
      cool mist. Let me speak plainly. Let me get to the dark

heart of the matter. The thing is, Love, that when I watch
      the squash buds wither, when the June sun makes them
shrivel into themselves, it's almost too much for me to bear.

      I see them—& that is all. I hear an emptiness in the wind,
& wrap my mind around it, & think of the king snake coiled
      in the grass. Soon he will be skin & bones. Already he is but

skin & bones. He rubs his head against a rock. The sun shines.
      Wood lice creep from the open dirt. Tonight, as the boy
turns in his bed, & wrestles with the prospect of his own

approaching dusk, I bend myself above you, or below, whichever
way it is that you prefer. I breathe the clean grasses
  of your skin & unpack each assorted item you keep hidden

in a travel sized box by your purse. And I, & the boy, sit
  blinking in the dark, staring off at the wall & the dead stars
beyond it throwing cold light through the black matter

  of millennia. It rests inside his palm. It rests in mine. At times,
looking out at the bare sky, & watching those stars fizzle
  in the map of still time, I want to crawl up into its stillness,

& feel obsolete, distant from my father & the warm bodies
  I've touched, & watch through a tree so lovingly hollowed
their vague shapes flit between leaves. It's a problem

  in philosophy & form, each hand's different twenty-
seven little bones reaching out to hold the cloth
  draped upon the shoulders of another. Slowly,

those shapes come into focus, & the dawn light, which is
  not dead light, seeps into the room. In it, in the yard,
where the boy throws down his spade, & a mule-tailed deer

  licks dew from his palm, the apple trees shine, collard
stalks stiffen, the paper-white bark of an aspen
  quivers, Love, & the grasses shudder in unison, in wind.

Peter Twal

On the Road

And when I awake   *Dear Diary,   Tuscaloosa: Death   came to me
last night, a couple exits early   cut my hair crooked in my sleep   So that's*

fine Snow beginning to stick   *a radio personality dying into a million pieces*
I read a book because people love their solitude   *in caves,*   *hello*
atop canyons, people sure it's their echoes saying
back when really it's their mothers drowning farther and farther away
Then I found a rest stop   *Then I ate the book,   feeling by feeling* The way we forget people

is piecewise   cutting them up and hiding the memories in our freezers   I take note: *today's
is the exact amount of times I can be yanked from myself   by some long oily arm from above
before I forget whether I am the arm or the toy soldier   the placeholder*

the excuse   I can't be sure but, in between strangled radio stations, a car backfiring
next to me or just an atom, miles away   splitting   Such is the life expectancy
of things,   shouts a billboard and a text message from you about finding my phantom limb
in the back seat of your car   Months later, I will text back   *thanks for that*

Patrick Errington
White Lies

Say the quiet grows around you, that the slip of light
is all that pins my hand to your chest when the senses quit
taking and start offering up the little blueabout, the little
stones they've culled from the riverbed. Say you're always

> *You, and a river's deepest turns promising your body*
> *a new shape, a way down. Orphan of water,*
> *step back onto the bent rocks, into*
> *the warming of me. There's too much sky,*
> *too much breathing to be done. You say I've never been*

small in these smallest rooms. Say sea. Say it backward
in my ear. Or stop and say there's nothing left but
the nest of rust, that your body is emptied of you—how
wide your eyes say you can say everything, wildly, out,

> *wrong enough to be forgiven or even to ask. Yet I bend,*
> *each night, to the sink as if to a nurse's hand,*
> *wait for the drought to wash me*
> *against the mirror. While you sleep, sometimes, I kneel*
> *on the cool tiles, hope they're white enough to take me in.*

like a Chinook arch of thunderhead, hurling itself
against a field of bent gold, of canola flowers and tar,
until at night it admits stars. Or like a deer, god-split
on the snow, giving out a language of paling clouds.

> *Snow might come, but not without a break or a body*
> *to collect against. If I could invent a word for a blank*
> *square of my wall, would that make it real?*
> *It can't exist, white, you told me. I've seen snow only*
> *from the shadows, said you by saying everything you are not.*

Its marrow sucked from the open ulna until it draws
crystals of cold to the muzzle. Say you said
it all, your colours to the coils of your finger pads,
what would you let light? Finches. Copper wire. Rome.
Caraway. You. Say this never happened.

Peter LaBerge
The Newcomers

for Melisa Gregory

Bodies are forests in this knot
of space. Unblemished, these roots—

I let my fingers wander where they may,
between the trees, call the world *mine*.

Morning slips between moments
of holy ice—*Sir, there was nothing we could do*

about the darkness. Because here, the sun
is born already slant. I trap this fissure of light

*

in my mouth so I will never forget
warm breath on cheeks, I do this as I record

the smell my body takes from dusk. Soon the sun
will lose itself to indigo once more, unsure

whether what remains is beaten in, ripped out—
by whom, even. Meanwhile, detectives huddle

under tarps by the woods—*Sir, we are doing*
everything we can do. There are rumors about death

I wish to debunk: first, you cannot gamble away
your skin. There is no false bottom

*

to the hearse that carries a corpse. Everyone turns
the same shade of early morning when lifeless, a color

that cannot be described, must be believed in. And it is
not an honor to find oneself where one is led—

it is early March in Iowa. Beneath these plains, I lack
a voice. I have only what I remember: welcoming

the still-soft roots, the unfed ice, the patient bale of hay.

Karl Zuehlke
Autumn

Forget all you know of winter.
        The father who disappears

as he walks across the field into cedars.
        Forget all you know of walking

on the moon—drifts, dunes, the wading.
        Wadding up paper and unfolding it.

White mountains. White oceans.
        Forget that. As a child I watched

my father lie in bed, hands crossed
        over his chest and white sheets

as if he were practicing for a grave.
        Under white oceans, white snow,

the moon is stone and will not hatch.
        When my father could hardly stand

but stood and sat a whole day with us.
        He said forget spring, forget rebirth.

All you have is all you have to lose.
        Forget forgetting, forget reprieve.

My turn to feel the swing of the moon.
        That ax cuts no shadow down.

Just me. I aim to give you what you
        cannot keep—a blue twice as true.

Autumn is the well from which you sing.
        These the stones, the knee deep water.

This well is my well and yours.
        You are the child beneath the ax.

Jessica Poli
Milkstone

Night wears your sweat
like an antlered buck

carrying moss.
Another wine glass breaks,

accidentally tapped
against the kitchen faucet.

Out in the dark,
a goat is bleating—

a milkstone
lodged in her udder.

The night flees on hooves.

Kenzie Allen
In Which I Become (Tiger Lily)

> *Why does he ask you, "How?"*
> *Once the Injun didn't know*
> *All the things that he know now*

The way back from the fire
was so long. Three canoes
worth of carving the trees

once I got that rope off.
I crackled, I snapped and
twisted and turned red

but was not also fire.
Once I did not know
the good medicine,

what month the strawberry
peeks up from the path,
which animals were clans

and not spirits, which spirits
for which we left the meal
outside the longhouse door,

once I did not know my name
though I knew the good cloth
they wrapped me in, the women

and their songs. It is in the fjords
Mother calls to me,
always en route, Facetimes

another BC, GTC,
blood discussion. I love a man
to Punnett squares, tear

my own teeth out on
unseen, know violence
like it made me. Rage

like it rocked me to sleep.
All I want in the world
is a jingle dress and a baby

with darker skin than mine.
These are not our lands
but the soil is good

for growing apples.
These are not our apples
but the flesh is good

and crisp. Sometimes
the rope was even
a comfort, like a bruise,

visible. Some nights
I wished for that from him.
But no one wishes

for the tongue-tie, lockjaw,
for the smoke signal to work
only one way. No one asks

the red woman what made her.
Once I did not know
and I asked, *how*

can one hurt a fire,
if the skin is already
bubbled and charred,

how can one wound
a wound, but it deepens,
with each new smile

I learn.

Kyle Dacuyan
Whalemouth

Inside the Whalemouth there is only
pure feeling. The animal plummets
and crashes with religious attention,
dutifully violent, like the beating free
of dust from an ancient rug.
If there is such a thing as soul
I will hold my breath through to it.
I will hold my breath until I am dead
or this is over, I told myself
when the stranger fucked me awake
outside a nightclub in Berlin. In, out,
the consciousness, the not—
and the whale wept me again
into existence, prone upon the pavement,
cheek pressed to my grit bed.
I remembered what a foreigner I was.
How stupid, how English and few
my words are. I walked half the morning
in a gridless part of town until I reached
the fake-poor flat I had been borrowing
from a slick junkie DJ. I knelt on all fours
in his shower like a humbled impostor
but could not clean enough inside myself,
could not deceive myself with dreaming
when I tried to sleep the day away.
I dreamt the dream called Whalemouth
I have had since early puberty at least—
Whalemouth, mammal I cannot claw

myself apart from, cavern I will need to light
with all my violent, bright attention—
Whalemouth, when I would wake paralyzed,
I used to believe that I was dying,
that dying was an interminable dream
of uselessness inside a room that never changes.
That dreams and life keep happening
in the same vulgar circle is the one
indication I have of my ability to rise.
And I did. I took the night bus from Berlin.
Ahead of me, a Turkish mother sang lullabies
to soothe her fearful child. I listened
for some time. When I woke, it was morning.
It was morning, and we had come together
to the edge of the Black Forest.

Mary-Alice Daniel
Mefloquine Side Effect #1: Nightmares

The first thing the dead might say
when they finally get a chance to respond

is:　　*Sing*!

(Terrible singing—terrible songs.)

The dead may be controversial—they may liken us to birds.
Maybe birds should just go a little wild.

Sometimes the spirit-like quality is pleasing and slight—
But every once in a while I want a little *muscle*—you know?

I don't yet feel the weight of these enormous birds,
because they're only wings and wings are only light.

Parrots do have a presence.
They have the quality of bad visitants—a dire nature in their speech.
Parrots remember your face—(*conspire*)—can find you.

A two-inch feather emerges
from a baby girl's neck:
the body internalizes
the flight-coded language of dreams.

Talin Tahajian
Remedies

You were the color of a dove & I don't know what to do
about that. I have never understood how to cup my hands

& take communion. Like a faithful daughter, I carry this
with me. I stab it with feathers & pray until it is covered

in gems. I rinse it in the river that knows my blood, wring
it out beneath a full moon. I know nothing about bird calls.

I know nothing about meat. Bless the river & all the fish
we poisoned. Foreign fluids. Bless the red birches forced

to watch. I want to burn something, so I char the flesh
of a catfish & think of myself. Girl as carp. Small tragedy

with freshwater pearls. I baptize myself in this water
& I see myself float in this water. Somewhere, a flock

of crows & I don't hear anything over the soft breath
of river fish as they touch me in places that don't exist.

Gaetan Sgro
This Life Is a Fox I Stole

—for Clovis "Butch" Ash

What will not make sense to those so fond
of combat: when my time comes I *will* go

gently. Despite my younger age, the still-
hard lines of my body, my faith, despite

the raw and fraying fibers of my being
for my family's sake I refuse

to betray this pain. For years I served
below decks assembling ordinances

addressing packages of Hellfire
delivered on blade-thin wings

of death. While in the darkness of that
dread machine reactors glowed and set

my marrow *free*— Though decades passed
before we named the beast. Like me

there was a boyish thief who kept a secret
pinned against his breast. And even

as the feral pup all snarl and claw and
starving bared its fangs and started

gnawing— Even as the wound outgrew
his slender frame the Spartan tightened

his embrace. Like him I love the light
no less for lack of raging. Would rather save

my breath and bear the teeth. After all this
life is a fox I stole, and foxes need to eat.

Jen Siraganian
Monroe, Washington

Wrapped in dampness, we are soil alive
with slugs and foxglove. Everything moves.

The previous tenants evicted, only
earthworms elongate across the screen.

We see life in moisture. We speak of a house
for chickens and horses for the stable,

but first we haul. Heavy with wet,
we sort hairless dolls, clothes sodden

with rot, a mattress burned to the coils.
Scrap metal in one pile, wood slats

in another, yogurt tubs and a rusted bike
in a third. Who knew that Lego spacemen

don't decompose? These piles are not
our own, but our work gloves dampen

through. All is wet, wet, wet. Snails
weave through ribbons of trash bags.

Three trips to Lowes for PVC piping
and copper caps, a doe sleeps behind

a blueberry bush. Peeling shelf mushrooms
from bark, I ask, *can we eat this kind?*

It's too tough, you say, *but it won't hurt you.*
You pluck crooked nails. We clear sadness

from the house, find florescent orthodontic bands
in the living room. That night, we curl into sleep.

Tomorrow, you whisper, *we'll fix the well,*
and I see our shower fill with steam.

Matthew Wimberley
Poem Ending with Infinity on the Glass

Out there, beyond the sleeping
rows of shagbark
the fog in the valley is as speechless
as the ice locking the water-wheel
to rest. Birdless sky—
there is an emptiness to it all
like the hunters in Bruegel's painting
watching skaters on a frozen lake
make figure eights with dulling blades.
I think of the glass eyes of angels
dark in the stone church
where my father is a smudge of ash
across my forehead. The snow falls
behind them. I have my father's
eyes and my mother's voice—his
truculence and her quiet. I don't know
what any of it's gotten me.
When I come back, as I had to,
to the little town empty handed—
a magician with only half
a trick—no one notices. The addicts
smoke cigarettes at the corner gas station
waiting for their dealer
to drive up in a busted Subaru wagon
and sell them some glass. The snow
keeps falling. Oblivious, lost in its pattern.
What happens when the last flake floats
out of the trees? What's left

to make a blankness I can drag
my pen through? In the church
the pastor pushes his thumb into my face
and says suffering is a condition
for forgiveness. Someone
told me my father did not suffer. In the end
death was instant. But nothing in this life
is instant. Once, at a café where we could sit
at a window and look out on the wet road
a friend explained infinity to me. He put
his lips close to the window and breathed
until he'd made a gray film on the glass.
With his index finger he cut
a line across it, with two vertical strokes
at each end where he drew the numbers
"0" and "1," then asked, "What is this?"
I said "The distance between zero and one."
"And," he lifted his hand, "what is half of this?"
He divided the line, then
again and again until I could see out past it—
to the snow galloping through itself
like laughter that could go on forever.

Cintia Santana
Notes to a Funeral

---

[1] According to the old law, the body must be buried within two days.

[2] Lit so that nothing looks like it's under glass, as in a museum.

[3] Compare "Those are pearls that were his eyes" (Shakespeare, *The Tempest*, I. ii. 398).

[4] "The world is terrifying" (Fr.). That is, despair, carrion comfort, feasts on her.

[5] A narrow passage between houses or, as here, rocks.

[6] The imperative, "Take," is understood here, though it does not appear until the next stanza.

[7] Originally, a dialogue in verse between two shepherds.

[8] Rice paddy. River and shrine. Rain (Jpn.). The imagery recalled contrasts with the growing threat of snow.

[9] Alludes to the scene in which the princess writes a letter and gives it to the page. The page sets off but cannot find the temple; he longs for the familiar capital.

[10] "In the end, you, too, will complete your assignment and, like me, return to the capital."

[11] *Nine Ways to Cross a River*, 179.

[12] Suite, famous for its intimate sarabande, the second of only four movements without chords. Tortelier describes it as an extension of silence.

[13] The imprint of his body in the grass.

[14] A memory that unfastens.

[15] "Under his breath" (It.).

[16] The full phrase asks, "Is man but a parable for God?"

[17] "We obey but we do not comply" (Sp.). Maxim with which the Guipuzcoans vetoed the laws of the Spanish sovereign.

[18] *Language as Gesture*, 1952, 352.

[19] Devotions, performed in memory.

[20] *Collected Poems (1927–2012).*

[21] "…swallowtails lift from the railway tie" (*Letters,* 120).

Alex Chertok

The Museo del Prado Closes Early on New Year's Eve

Madrid, Spain

Pity the tourists. They've come for Velasquez's
Las Meninas and get only the painting's
bottom right, only the girl and her mastiff
patient forever under the brushstroke
of the museum guard's arm pointing them back.

Pity the tourists rifling through their words,
their *Por favor* and *Pintura.* Pity them,
who'll never learn what shadows really are:
dark blues and the reds of hemangiomas,
never black. Or the lemon pith of light.

Pity their *Dejame* tangled with the hostage prayer
they were told stateside to learn,
Bismillah al-rahman al-rahim,
two-tongued for how heavy the syllables
and how far they are from faith. *In the name
of God, the Beneficent, the Merciful.*

Pity the tourists, lost in fear's hundred floors,
each with a hundred wings. They can only get
so close: pity their inching forward, their waiting
for the world to snipe its shrill alarm at them.

Bismillah, Let-me-live, I'm-one-of-
you, held in their mouths as the suited
and name-tagged one herds them out like captives.
Pity them, who believe this Velazquez

still is theirs. They know it now. They know it
as well as the pigeon that nests on the basilica
knows what sacred is. The way they know all of Spain,
having breathed its air for ten days straight, or
a whole song from a single pilfered line. They've seen
the painting, they'll say—pity them—as they'd see

a swatted moth's whole life from the death-dust
its wings leave on the window. Or as they'd see
a firefly between flashes in the dark of night
that is not black. Nothing is. And nothing's white.

Rachel Michelle Hanson
Bound

We hid our indiscretion in a truck bed,
though the stars knew. At first I tucked closer
to the red metal of the Ford than your body,
trying so hard to be good. I felt that cold band
around your finger, your hand atop mine,
it's what kept my kisses short. On the river you
were gentle, lacked insistence. Let me keep to myself.
And from the back of the boat I watched you, moving
calm and lovely, tall and thin amongst black rocks—
the Vishnu Shist, and hot sand. Sometimes I gasp against
longing for space not mine, a selfish desire to see you
in front of me, unhitched, your fingertips
softly playing at my calf.

Benjamin Goodney
To Lack the Concept Ecstasy

I long
held to my belief in seashells
though I no longer have eyes
to see with, nor coracles to listen for
murmurs on the other side of the wall.

Valves pump
through veinless waves this weak
magnetic field seeking the smelt again
like a missing limb,
my iron-tasting shore.

Bareknuckle conch
envies the jellyfish its comet tail,
spiral-petaled id
its armature the distant spheres
breathing polyrhythmic.

Brainless life
deserves its length of rope
nets drawn up by odd-fingered driftwood
hands whose rough desire is to drown
and in the air caress me.

Alyssa Jewell
Frida Kahlo Takes a Muse in Detroit

after her smallest self-portrait

1.

And I was only half in this life, withered beneath the stink
of sour milk mop, legs like paperclips unwound then bound
into sculpture: a brass tree rooted to the kitchen table, branched hands
arced beyond a milk saucer skyline bent of plaster. But the truth is,
had you been next to me all along, I'd have stretched green and peach plum pear
beautiful, round hayfield, and moon-drenched lovely for you.
I'd be the keeper of the dew and kick down the frost.

2.

You on ladders, you finding balance on the highest branch thick
with apples tumbling like red stones into bucket—I saw you there
speaking in a language only I could hear and wondered
who you'd feed with all that sugar in your hands. Would you
toss a layer of flesh to the evening sidewalk to lighten your load, then shake
October's dust and the horizon's naked trees from your shoulders
before going home? O my hunger, little greed to green my copper toes.

3.

I'd hide my bus-wrecked bones for you, shattered pelvis out of frame
and only reveal stars for eyes sly and brighter in the darkest part
of the landscape as if to say, there's a whole drawbridge left to unhinge
in the corner of my mouth, point of vanishing, point of the holy unspoken and no
return. Jean Harlow and all her angels couldn't sing to me tonight, couldn't

bring back the kidnapped or the dead or the nipped with a knife. My skull
beats with shadows and light, the concentric blooms of a conch shell
          winding off the page.

Susannah B. Mintz
Anti-eclogue

I woke up to the cat eating the phone. Poised on the edge of the bed like a little yogini.

My friend calls to tell me she's having an affair with a married woman. Then my father calls to say he's reading *The Brothers Karamazov*. He's a big Dostoevsky fan now, can't get enough of the murder and betrayal. Later in the day a student complains, "it's always about sex," and "if you walked around thinking everyone was fixated on sex like Freud says they are, it would just be so funny."

When I was a kid I'd go to the woods to smoke cinnamon sticks. The exact length and girth of a cigarette but of course they don't draw, so pulling too hard makes you lose your breath. October brings it back to me: the smell of wood fire, the color of wet. It's the cruelest month, with all due respect—a month of anniversaries I'd rather not mark, and now, last in the chain, a year since the day that was meant to redeem a season but took the other way instead. Fall in the fullest sense of the word, transgressions and falling in love and falling apart and falling down drunk. You fall to your knees. You fall flat on your face. A shadow falls across the page. A wisp of hair falls into your eyes. I once sang Patsy Kline's "I Fall to Pieces" to a friend for his birthday. He laughed at first but when he realized I was seriously serenading him, he got a look of wonder on his face and I could see him come to his senses, literally, as an act of mindfulness. Later I fell for a guy because he showed me phlox in the real world, because he made them real, not the shibboleth of poets like *timothy* or *light*.

My grandmother died in October, and my first love left, and then another, and one more. Losses that stack up like couch cushions. Bereft: to be robbed of a loved one. To be plundered in love.

When I rolled over to answer the phone (it was him calling, the man of phlox and sweet William and broom) the cat fell off the bed, making a mewling sound. And that's why I proposed to him—because of course, internal gyroscope and all, cats don't fall so much as twist. Because we came home one night to a toad on the front walk and he knew it wasn't a frog. Because they're both right, Freud and my student—that desire, like pain, reduces everything to itself, and if we didn't find that a little bit funny, we'd fall over backward under the strain of our wishing. Waterfalls. Falling stars.

Jeremy Allan Hawkins
You Must Become a Bear

to reveal your intelligence
in the village you crush clay pots
seeking out tulip bulbs

you pull koi from the pond
& after dark you stalk
those who stray
beyond the house lights

to show you know how
you will feed on anything

to adapt yourself to the climate
of the people's observations
you will be either totem or omen

the spirit of their fears
or a sign of the gift
demanded by the wilderness
to honor its abundance

either one written in dark
splashes across the meadow

in the long summer
you will not feel sorrow
even into autumn's stately walk
feasting on gourd fields

& gorging on fallen apples
until you are dizzy

when the first chill blows
up from a ravine
glazed early with frost
across the orchard grass
& you will scent it again

that enduring odor of yourself
only as escapable as living

to which you are resigned
as you trudge out of the village
up to the ravine
in search of a crevice
where the next step must lead you
into the forgetfulness of sleep
your guilt there
the subject of a fearful dream

Kaveh Akbar
Fugu

the liver of a blowfish is said to
be the tastiest part   it's also the
most toxic an ounce enough to kill ten
men   I have avoided it completely
which is not to say I've been unreckless
as a boy I saw a wolf in the shade

of a yew tree   I stared   it stared at my
staring   I whispered *banam-e-khudah*
it bolted   it could have shredded me like
a paper kite in a storm   I used to
believe my father's umbrella caused the
rain   he was so powerful   nobody
has turned out to be as powerful as
I believed my father to be   least of
all my father with his insulin and
heart medication   now he can't even
eat the fruit he grows which doesn't stop him
from growing it   he dries it sends boxes
of pressed quince apple cherry peach pear plum

that I struggle to love other men is
a lie I've uttered with confidence at
certain convenient moments in my life
I can't imagine anything less true
now with the dizzying sweet fruit still stuck
in my teeth   my gums and tongue tinted green
a quiet question answering itself

Rachel Inez Lane

Dear Bat Boy,

I've followed your career for some time
        now, mainly in the grocery store,
                after being shooed away by couples

from the wine and cheese aisle—
        or while waiting in line with the kind of parents
                who'd let their rotten taters totter up

and laugh in your face as you screamed, because
        you cling to a visceral world
                that refuses to understand you!

Or, so I've read, in the *Weekly World News*. Oh,
        they only focused on your faults—
                "Bat Boy! Drunk on Party Boat—"

"Bat Boy Bites Santa Claus—"
        They mistook your passion
                for aggression then romanticized

it later—"Bat Boy Searches for Love—"
        tried softening you up, but you're no donut,
                you're half-bat, half-boy

who, according to scientists,
        has a confused sense of morality—
                as is mine,

according to my ex, who said, *It's not that I don't like*
    you, I just don't like what you do.
        Like, I'm trouble? I said. *Yeah,*

he said, *like that*...Squares, Bat Boy, have angles
    I'll never understand,
        but a bat has a heart

the size of its body, so I can see why
    you went off the grid and live in tunnels now.
        I imagine the reason some of us go

underground is to gain access to that dark piece
    of something everyone else
        has overlooked, and once they find

a way inside they leave nothing
    but footprints behind. I can see that
        on cold nights

when the sky gets misty-eyed,
    lit windows warm outlines—
        and there is so much love outside

my brick apartment, it's almost too much
    to take—I can feel the breathing
        of the half-opened mouth

alarm bell, a train glides by—
    all I can see are bones I can't
        hold hard enough—

because I'm all nerves.
    My heart is a pipe bomb
        in anyone's hands.

Stephanie Cawley
Mary Shelley

A glossy paragraph for names whispered in the dark.
Did you have anywhere you were hoping to travel?
A novel all scenes of sailboats, horseback, countryside
panorama. Seventeen names for what the mouth
does, all translating to *open*. Under *throat*, see sea-shells
spelled out to a coast. Under *hold*, see wide sky
where birds keep appearing. If you put a freckled
shoulder against your lips, don't expect it to remember.

*

Down to the essentials of down parka, fur
boots, eggs white and cold. A novel all scenes
of unzippering. To do in the dark where birds
keep flocking: remember, let go, keep
from disappearing. Your tongue, in particular, stopped
a throat whistling, a kettle on the stove,
a letter home. Do you like, as I do, a camera with no
film, sky floating blue and glossy across a lens?

*

Scars are only so long unless scrubbed with lemon
and sugar. A panorama of sailboats, each
whispered name a horse in your mouth. I mean,
first I had to stop wanting to hold on
to everything. To stitch a scene with fence posts,
white bones, gold zippers. Teeth

in a mouth, open like no answers, no questionable
temperatures. Shoulders, no no, no, etcetera.

Craig Beaven
One-Hundred-Years Meditation

Amy is still asleep. In all my days of living here
the radon fans have never stopped turning. Clouds form
in the rocks where our house
was built. We must be free of this cloud, which would rise
through the floorboards and be breathed. Maybe there's no where
good to live. Under gray all the time in the north, beneath clouds
coming in for Halloween, snow until Easter.
Texas, the soil was clay and clay shifts
with heat and rain, house inching, cracks
on every wall. The engineers
said the structure was sound. *If the tree out front dies*
they mentioned in passing,
the house will collapse as the roots decay. But that may be
in a hundred years. They dug out under the dining room
and with a hydraulic press raised the slab four inches, setting it
level again. Here, we breathe in and out
and down below the home the littlest fan takes
all the air that comes up from the rock and pushes it
into the grass, into the camellias, up into the wind and the trees.
We have to live somewhere. The blades turning as the night turns
and the little bags at the end of our lungs inflate.
Who discovered radon, or that it seeps into houses, invisible
and odorless? We take it on faith. Our realtor said
you would have to live here a hundred years before you felt
the effects—so who has ever felt it? Has died from the rock
fifteen feet below? Gravity pulls it and the squeeze
cracks it and the cracks release air that's been inside
for a million years. The clock ticks and the fan hums. The birds

are still; no branch moves or leaf turns. Everyone will be up soon. I know
some are already up and some have not yet slept. The breathing
is imperceptible. I don't know what lungs are made of,
it isn't flesh and it isn't bone. I know the sacs at the ends of lungs
are named for the Greek god of wind, who blew around Odysseus,
who kept the story going with breath. Today is the future.
Here it comes: blue, between black
leaves. Every second is bluer. I know behind me
it's white at the fence line. The fan down at the bottom
is no longer audible
but it's there and goes on turning
saving our future lives.

Moriah Cohen

Snow Downgraded to Nuisance on the Narrow Street

Houses wake with light by the mug-full—
parades of underarmor and boots; cars
backfire then shimmy to a start.

The second time
we're born they say will be of fire.

The third of snow.

But coaxing the boy's
arms through his sleeves, the woman knows
this time he was born an elephant which is
to say he is an obelisk and a rope.

Just last night, she woke to the radio
looping a station's jingle followed by
militants dragging a foreign city by its
spindly legs.

She turned on the lamp. Or she didn't.

She swaddled her little elephant in wet
darkness that branched like pines
that ring the house.

These hours fray at the tips,
peal or tip-toe, want what they want, if only bodies
to knead the swollen mouth, massage

from the pain a shape as she coaxes them
through sleep.

Dali's joke: the animal does not know
where it ends nor begins.

And there is something swanlike about that,
isn't there? A beauty that hurts so bad
in its understanding of its own loneliness.

Once, she saw a cygnet spill across the confusion
of a white lake.

At water's center rested an island.
On the island, black trunks blanching at the tips.

Cara Dees
Vigil Hemming In

Lightless light and my father's cigarette

smoke softening into it and the light
complicit with the smoke and softening, too,

into the field's hitherto horizon, the field

a blur of turned drumlin. A flick of ash
and a mottled dove melts into the failing hickory.

So this is the sunset with you removed—

a circle withdrawing into a deeper circumference,
and so on. Then some. When you were,

light knew its home and kept within it.

Names held their course. Each poem chose
one headstrong color and became it utterly,

not like this blownback space, this all-

over sound, where *petal* can mean *mare pressed
to ground*, can mean *little girl lost, little woman

stormbound*. Words need edges to survive. Or else,

this hickory and its gathering of doves, this everywhere-
song, this widower burning behind the window.

Benjamin Garcia
Le Daría Mis Pulmones

Toward the end, she could only
lift a cup of coffee. Closer still,
even that became too much for her,
my mother. A sponge, then,
I'd dip in coffee, or dip *pan dulce*,
and put that to her lips to suck. That
was all the cancer let her manage.

The IV was her sugar water, and she
the hummingbirds she loved to watch,
busy at the red and yellow feeder.
Those plastic flowers welded on
were poor excuses, but they worked. Whatever

worked, I guess, my mother thought,
lived. On the bed in the living room,
her body of sleeping birds, her dream
of a thousand green wings shimmering like
shreds of aluminum, that could, at any moment,
unloose on the wind. Toward

the end, the sponge and the coffee, the cancer.
She couldn't smoke anymore either, of course,
because even drawing her own drag: impossible.
So she had me smoke for her—nine years old—
I was her lungs. I blew the smoke right in her face, right
in her face. Just like that, over and over:

L.S. McKee
Alva and the Complex Pool

You see, sooner or later, everything falters
into radiance. The smallest components of our pent-up

contingencies ignite. Energy shimmers in every cell.
This afternoon, for example, from the balcony

of my condo, in which I have lived exactly
three years, and which overlooks the liner-blue water

of the complex pool, I watched a boy dive.
It was half past noon. I'd been left waiting for someone

to arrive. And though this has always been the case,
I felt no hurry as the boy's body marked time like

a clock hand hiccupping again into motion.
After a long dormancy, there is often a mechanical gasp,

followed by a faint smell of smoke because dust kindles
under the grinding gears. But I was not burning exactly.

As I said, I was only waiting, which, let's face it,
is a kind of fire, but smaller. One rule of nuclear physics:

in collapse there is light. Energy, like a rejected lover,
has to go somewhere. To stay is an impossibility.

The water will ripple no matter how precisely
you enter it, no matter how carefully you climb

from its depths, as when the boy hoisted himself up
the ladder, detonating waves that could not find him.

—Nominated by *The Georgia Review*

Christine G. Adams
The Root Systems of Orchids

What they need more
than water is air.
      When I eddy in a life
it is as a rushing current rather than
a whirling,
      fog-rich gust. And so
the yellowing creeps from leaves,
to stem, to labellum,
      from the Latin for lip.

It is hard not to imagine the way
each man has turned
      his face
      away from me in the end
as the upward curl of a sepal.
      The gesture
that precedes the slow,
      caving-in of bloom.

I have soaked the velamen. Say it again,
velamen, velamen, velamen.
      The orchid—
          from the Greek word
for testicle, because
      of subterranean twin tubers
that feed the visible body—has nothing
left to nourish it
      from below the soil.

Everything has rotted. And still I fill
the watering can—
      always unable
to believe that others do not wake
      to only thirst.

Pireeni Sundaralingam

Fugue: Sri Lankan Civil War

—after Paul Celan

We were born, we were named,
we were schoolgirls dressed in white cotton.

There were bells, there were lessons, the light
a mirror, breaking over the lagoon.

We learned dates, we learned names,
we tied up our braids with long ribbons.

We see soldiers, we see checkpoints,
our brothers trapped between sandbags,
the drum roll of boats across the lagoon.

There are bells, there are lessons,
we march in white lines
and the priest takes our confession.

We learn dates, we learn names,
fill kerosene in bottles, douse the white cotton.
We are schoolgirls in white, our braids in long ribbons.

We are suspects, we are names,
we are women sheathed in white cotton,
the bells in the schoolyard,
bodies wrapped in white cotton.

We were born, we were named,
we were schoolgirls dressed in white cotton.
We tied up our braids and wove them with ribbons.

Jackson Holbert
Elegy

Many times I have chosen
the gar breathing on the river's back
the cottonmouth wide-eyed and crazy
above the blinding sky

of its mouth. Night carves the Arkansas autumn.
I have been with you always.
You stare and then
we stare together. What work

has not been done by looking
hard at something? You knock
your boot on a headstone
and I ring like a bell.

I mean to say—
I went into the river.
Inside it was a tree.
The tree fell.

Acknowledgments

Kaveh Akbar's "Fugu" originally appeared in *Gulf Coast*.

Kenzie Allen's "In Which I Become (Tiger Lily)" originally appeared in *Four Winds Magazine*.

Jo Brachman's "The Scientist's Hypothesis of Distance" originally appeared in *Cimarron Review*.

Anders Carlson-Wee's "To the Fingerless Man in Banff" originally appeared in *West Branch*.

Stephanie Cawley's "Mary Shelley" originally appeared in *Prelude*.

Sam Cha's "Word Problem: Heart" originally appeared in *The Missouri Review*.

Moriah Cohen's "Snow Downgraded to Nuisance on the Narrow Street" originally appeared in *Adroit Journal*.

Kyle Dacuyan's "Whalemouth" originally appeared in *The Shallow Ends*.

Mary-Alice Daniel's "Mefloquine Side Effect #1: Nightmares" originally appeared in *Hayden's Ferry Review*.

Nandini Dhar's "A Brief History of Clamor" originally appeared in *West Branch*.

Patrick James Errington's "White Lies" originally appeared in *Cider Press Review*.

Ariel Francisco's "Meditation on Patience" originally appeared in *Fjords Review*.

Benjamin Garcia's "Le Daría Mis Pulmones" originally appeared in *Kenyon Review Online*.

Julian Gewirtz's "The Gang's All Here" originally appeared in *Ploughshares*.

Wren Hanks's "The Ghost Incites a Genderqueer Pledge of Allegiance" originally appeared in *Gigantic Sequins*.

Rachel Michelle Hanson's "Bound" originally appeared in *New Madrid: Journal of Contemporary Literature*.

Jeremy Allan Hawkins's "You Must Become a Bear" originally appeared in *FOLDER*.

Jen Jabaily-Blackburn's "Braintree" originally appeared in *The Common*.

John James's "Poem Around Which Everything Is Structured" originally appeared in *Meridian*.

Alyssa Jewell's "Frida Kahlo Takes a Muse in Detroit" originally appeared in *Grist*.

Peter LaBerge's "The Newcomers" originally appeared in *Hayden's Ferry Review*.

Rachel Inez Lane's "Dear Bat Boy," originally appeared in *The Normal School*.

L.S. McKee's "Alva and the Complex Pool" originally appeared in *The Georgia Review*.

Joy Priest's "Ode to Hushpuppy" originally appeared in *Winter Tangerine Review*.

Jody Rambo's "Elegy in Which My Mother Learns to Swim" originally appeared in *Ruminate Magazine*.

Cintia Santana's "Notes to a Funeral" originally appeared in *The Threepenny Review*.

Caitlin Scarano's "Mule" originally appeared in *Radar Magazine*.

Charif Shanahan's "Song" originally appeared in *The Baffler*.

Pireeni Sundaralingam's "Fugue" originally appeared in *American Poetry Review*.

Talin Tahajian's "Remedies" originally appeared in *Indiana Review*.

Peter Twal's "On the Road" originally appeared in *RHINO*.

Contributors' Notes

CHRISTINE G. ADAMS received her MFA from The University of North Carolina at Greensboro where she was awarded the Fred Chappell Fellowship and served as poetry editor for *The Greensboro Review*. She is the recipient of two Academy of American Poets Prizes and her work appeared in *Best New Poets 2014*. She is currently a PhD candidate in poetry at Ohio University.

KAVEH AKBAR is the founding editor of *Divedapper*. His poems appear recently in *Poetry, APR, Tin House, PBS NewsHour*, and elsewhere. His debut collection, *Calling a Wolf a Wolf*, will be published in fall 2017 by Alice James Books. A 2016 recipient of the Ruth Lilly and Dorothy Sargent Fellowship from the Poetry Foundation, Kaveh was born in Tehran, Iran, and currently lives and teaches in Florida.

KENZIE ALLEN is a descendant of the Oneida Tribe of Indians of Wisconsin, and she is a graduate of the Helen Zell Writers' Program at the University of Michigan. Her work has appeared in *Drunken Boat, The Iowa Review, Apogee, Narrative, Boston Review*, and other venues, and she is the recipient of Hopwood Awards in poetry and nonfiction. She was born in West Texas, and can be found at kenzieallen.co.

A Kentucky native, CRAIG BEAVEN earned an MFA from Virginia Commonwealth University and a PhD from the University of Houston. His poetry manuscripts, currently in circulation, have been a finalist for thirteen different contests including the National Poetry Series, the Four Way Books Levis Prize, the Brittingham/Pollack Prizes, and many others. He lives with his wife and children in Tallahassee, Florida.

JENNY BOYCHUK holds an MFA in poetry from the University of Michigan's Helen Zell Writers' Program, where she is currently a Zell Fellow. Her poems have appeared in *Prairie Fire, Room, The Pinch, Salt Hill, Birdfeast, Elsewhere Mag*, and others.

JO BRACHMAN's work appears in *Poet Lore, Bellingham Review, Birmingham Poetry Review, Poetry East, Moon City Lit Review, The Southern Poetry Anthology* by Texas Review Press, *Waccamaw Literary Journal, Town Creek Poetry, San Pedro River Review, Tar River Poetry, Cimarron Review*, and *Terminus*. She is a recent fellow of the Hambidge Center for the Creative Arts and Sciences. She attends the low-residency MFA Creative Writing Program at Pacific University in Portland, Oregon, and lives near Atlanta, Georgia.

ANDERS CARLSON-WEE is a 2015 NEA Creative Writing Fellow and the author of *Dynamite*, winner of the 2015 Frost Place Chapbook Prize. His work has appeared in *Ploughshares, New England Review, AGNI, Poetry Daily, The Iowa Review, The Missouri Review, The Best American Nonrequired Reading*, and *Narrative Magazine*, which featured him on its 30 Below 30 list of young writers to watch. Winner of *Ninth Letter's* Poetry Award, *Blue Mesa Review's* Poetry Prize, and *New Delta Review's* Editors' Choice Prize, he was runner-up for the 2016 Discovery/Boston Review Poetry Prize. His work is currently being translated into Chinese. He lives in Minneapolis, where he's a 2016 McKnight Foundation Creative Writing Fellow.

STEPHANIE CAWLEY is from southern New Jersey. She is an MFA candidate at the University of Pittsburgh, and her poems have recently appeared or are forthcoming in the PEN Poetry Series, *TYPO, H_NGM_N, The Adroit Journal, Birdfeast*, and elsewhere.

SAM CHA writes: Aiyana Jones is real. The letter she wrote is real. I wrote this poem the day after the announcement of the Ferguson grand jury decision.

ALEX CHERTOK has work published or forthcoming in *The Missouri Review*, *The Cincinnati Review*, *Willow Springs*, *The Journal*, *Quarterly West*, *Copper Nickel*, and *Hayden's Ferry Review*, among others. He was awarded a fellowship to the Virginia Center for the Creative Arts, and completed his MFA degree at Cornell University, where he was also a Lecturer. He currently teaches at Ithaca College and through the Cornell Prison Education Program.

MORIAH COHEN is an instructor at The Academy for Information Technology in Union County, New Jersey. Her poetry has appeared in *Mid-American Review*, *Adroit Journal*, *Hayden's Ferry Review*, and *Narrative*, where she took second place in the 2013 30 Below Contest. She holds an MFA from Rutgers University–Newark. She lives with her two sons.

WILL CORDEIRO has work appearing in *Copper Nickel*, *Crab Orchard Review*, *DIAGRAM*, *Fourteen Hills*, *Valparaiso Poetry Review*, and else-where. He received his MFA and PhD from Cornell University. He lives in Flagstaff, where he teaches in the Honors Program at Northern Arizona University. This poem is inspired by, as well as dedicated to, Anders and Kai Carlson-Wee.

KYLE DACUYAN's work has been published in *Crab Orchard Review*, *THRUSH*, *RHINO*, and other journals. He lives in Brooklyn and serves as associate director of the Antiquarian Booksellers' Association of America.

MARY-ALICE DANIEL was born in northern Nigeria and raised in London, England, and Nashville, Tennessee. After attending Yale University, she received her MFA in poetry from the University of Michigan as a Rackham Merit Fellow. Her poems have received three Pushcart Prize nominations and have appeared or are forthcoming in *American Poetry Review*, *New England Review*, *Black Warrior Review*, *The Iowa Review*, *Hayden's Ferry Review*, *Callaloo*, and several anthologies. In 2016, she was a finalist for the Soros Fellowship for New Americans as well as for the Brunel University International African Poetry Prize. Her adopted home is Los Angeles, where she is completing her debut full-length poetry manuscript and earning a PhD in English literature and creative writing as an Annenberg Fellow at the University of Southern California.

JESSE DE ANGELIS lives in Boston. Previous poems have appeared in *Bird's Thumb, Glacial Erratic, The Kenyon Review, and Storm Cellar.*

CARA DEES holds an MFA degree from Vanderbilt University and teaches at Fisk University. She is the recipient of an Academy of American Poets Prize from the University of Wisconsin–Madison, a scholarship from the Sewanee Writers' Conference, a Pushcart Prize nomination, and was a finalist for *Indiana Review*'s 2016 Poetry Prize. Her work appears or is forthcoming in *The Adroit Journal, Beloit Poetry Journal, diode poetry journal, The Journal, Southern Humanities Review*, and elsewhere.

NANDINI DHAR is the author of the book *Historians of Redundant Moments* (Agape Editions). She divides her time between Miami, Florida, and Kolkata, India, and co-edits the online journal *Elsewhere* (www.elsewherlit.org) and the bi-lingual journal and micropress *Aainanagar*.

PATRICK JAMES ERRINGTON is a poet and translator from the prairies of Alberta, Canada. His poetry won *The London* Magazine 2016 Poetry Prize and has been featured in magazines and journals such as *The Iowa Review, West Branch, Cider Press Review, The Adroit Journal, DIAGRAM, Horsethief,* and others. A graduate of Columbia University's MFA program, Patrick currently lives in Scotland where he is a doctoral researcher and Buchanan scholar at the University of St Andrews.

ARIEL FRANCISCO is a first generation American poet of Dominican and Guatemalan descent. He is currently completing his MFA at Florida International University where he is the editor-in-chief of *Gulf Stream.*

His chapbook, *Before Snowfall, After Rain*, is available from Glass Poetry Press and his first full-length collection, *All My Heroes Are Broke*, is forthcoming from C&R Press. He lives in South Florida.

BENJAMIN GARCIA is the son of Mexican immigrants. He is a CantoMundo fellow who completed his MFA at Cornell University. He has received scholarships to attend the Bread Loaf Writers' Conference and the Taos Summer Writers' Conference. His work has appeared or is forthcoming in As/Us, Gulf Coast, KROnline, West Branch Wired, *The Collagist*, and PANK. He works for a nonprofit organization providing HIV/STD and opioid overdose prevention education to higher risk communities throughout New York's Finger Lakes region.

JULIAN GEWIRTZ's poems have been published by *AGNI, Boston Review, The Nation, The New Republic,* and the *Yale Review*. His poetry criticism and nonfiction essays have appeared in *The Economist*, the *Washington Post*, the *Los Angeles Review of Books*, and *VICE* magazine. She is on the web at www.juliangewirtz.com.

BENJAMIN GOODNEY's poems appear or are forthcoming in *Hotel Amerika, Seneca Review, Portland Review, Permafrost, Prick of the Spindle, Pacifica, Confrontation, Guernica,* and elsewhere. He co-founded and is managing editor of the literary magazine *Storm Cellar*. He took two degrees in philosophy from Illinois and resides along the Minneapolis–Orlando corridor.

WREN HANKS is the author of the chapbooks *Ghost Skin* (Porkbelly Press) and *Prophet Fever* (Hyacinth Girl Press). A 2016 Lambda Emerging Writers Fellow, their work appears in *Arcadia, Gigantic Sequins, Bone Bouquet, Drunken Boat, Permafrost,* and elsewhere. They are an associate editor for Sundress Publiwcations and live in Brooklyn.

RACHEL MICHELLE HANSON has published poems and prose in *The Iowa Review, New Madrid, Best of the Net 2015, Creative Nonfiction, The South Dakota Review, American Literary Review, The Minnesota Review, Entropy Magazine*, and elsewhere. In the summers she runs the Colorado River, which is the inspiration for her newest hybrid work in progress. She holds a PhD in nonfiction from the University of Missouri.

JEREMY ALLAN HAWKINS was born in New York City and raised in the Hudson Valley. He is an alumnus of the Fulbright U.S. Student Program and was a recipient of a teaching fellowship from the Alabama Prison Arts + Education Project. He is the author of *A Clean Edge*, selected by Richard Siken as the winner of the 2016 BOAAT Chapbook Prize, forthcoming in 2017. He lives in France.

JACKSON HOLBERT is originally from eastern Washington and is currently an undergraduate at Brandeis University in Waltham, Massachusetts. His work has appeared or is forthcoming in *The New Orleans Review, Tupelo Quarterly, Thrush,* and *the minnesota review*, among others.

JEN JABAILY-BLACKBURN's recent work has appeared in *The Common, cream city review, Cimarron Review,* and is forthcoming in *Massachusetts Review*. Her poem "For Gene Kelly" appeared in *Best New Poets 2014*. She lives in western Massachusetts with her husband and daughter, and is the administrative assistant for the Poetry Center at Smith College.

JOHN JAMES is the author of *Chthonic*, winner of the 2014 CutBank Chapbook Award. His poems appear or are forthcoming in *Boston Review, Kenyon Review, West Branch, Crazyhorse, Gulf Coast, Best New Poets 2013,* and elsewhere. He holds an MFA in poetry from Columbia University, where he held multiple fellowships and received an Academy of American Poets Prize. He is completing an MA in English at Georgetown University, where he serves as graduate associate to the Lannan Center for Poetics and Social Practice.

ALYSSA JEWELL studies poetry at Western Michigan University where she served as assistant editor for *New Issues Poetry and Prose* and is currently poetry editor for *Third Coast*. Her work has appeared or is forthcoming in *Chautauqua, Cider Press Review, The Columbia Review, Cumberland River Review, Dunes Review, Fifth Wednesday, Grist, Painted Bride Quarterly*, and *Pittsburgh Poetry Review*, among other journals. She lives and teaches in Grand Rapids.

PETER LABERGE is the author of the chapbooks *Makeshift Cathedral* (YesYes Books, 2017) and *Hook* (Sibling Rivalry Press, 2015). His recent work appears in *Beloit Poetry Journal, Best New Poets 2014, Harvard Review, Indiana Review, Iowa Review*, and *Pleiades*, among others. He is the recipient of a fellowship from the Bucknell University Stadler Center for Poetry and the founder and editor-in-chief of *The Adroit Journal*. He lives in Philadelphia, where he is an undergraduate student at the University of Pennsylvania.

RACHEL INEZ LANE is a Nashville-based poet and writer. Her work has appeared in *LA Review, Rattle, Nimrod, Mississippi Review, The Normal School*, and *Ploughshares*.

JENNIE MALBOEUF is a native of Kentucky. Her poems are found in the *Virginia Quarterly Review, Oxford Poetry, The Hollins Critic, Epoch, New American Writing, Hunger Mountain, New South*, and elsewhere. She lives in North Carolina and teaches writing at Guilford College.

MAX MCDONOUGH is a Creative Writing Fellow at Vanderbilt University. He grew up on the Jersey Shore.

L.S. MCKEE's poetry has appeared in *The Georgia Review, Crazyhorse, Birmingham Poetry Review, Blackbird, Ninth Letter, Gulf Coast, Indiana Review, New South, B O D Y, Oversound*, and elsewhere. She received her MFA from the University of Maryland and a Wallace Stegner Fellowship from Stanford University. Originally from East Tennessee, she lives in Atlanta and teaches at the University of West Georgia.

Susannah B. Mintz is a professor of English at Skidmore College. She is the author of the Kindle Single "Match Dot Comedy" (Amazon 2013) and winner of the 2014 South Loop National Essay Prize. A collection titled *Paper Cranes: 3 Essays* was a finalist for the *Epiphany* chapbook contest in 2015. Her creative nonfiction has appeared in *The Writer's Chronicle, Birmingham Poetry Review, Epiphany, Ninth Letter, Life Writing, Michigan Quarterly Review, Sycamore Review, Puerto del Sol,* and elsewhere. She was a finalist for the 2010 William Allen nonfiction prize and received a Notable Essay mention in the 2010 *Best American Essays.* She is also the author of three scholarly monographs and co-editor of a collection of critical work on the essayist Nancy Mairs. She is currently at work on an edited collection, *Unplotted Stories.*

Elizabeth O'Brien lives in Minneapolis, Minnesota, where she earned an MFA in poetry at the University of Minnesota. Her poetry and prose has appeared in many journals, including *New England Review, The Rumpus, Diagram, Sixth Finch, Radar Poetry, PANK, Cicada,* and the *Ploughshares* blog. Her chapbook, *A Secret History of World Wide Outage,* is forthcoming from ELJ Editions.

Erick Piller received an MFA in poetry from Warren Wilson College in 2012. His writing has appeared in *TriQuarterly, DIAGRAM, H_NGM_N, Fugue, Alice Blue,* and elsewhere. He lives in Danielson, Connecticut, and is pursuing a PhD in rhetoric and composition and creative writing pedagogy at the University of Connecticut.

Jessica Poli is the author of the chapbooks *Alexia* (Sixth Finch), *Glassland* (JMWW), and *The Egg Mistress* (Gold Line Press). Her work has appeared or is forthcoming in *The Adroit Journal, Caketrain,* and *Southern Indiana Review,* among others. She is a graduate of Syracuse University's MFA program, and the editor of *Birdfeast.*

Joy Priest is a poet from Louisville, Kentucky, and winner of the 2016 Hurston/Wright Foundation's College Writers Award. She has received scholarships from the Fine Arts Work Center at Provincetown, the Bread Loaf Writers' Conference, and the University of South Carolina where she is currently an MFA candidate. Her poetry and prose has been published or is upcoming in *The New Yorker, Blackbird, Callaloo, Drunken Boat, espnW, Muzzle, Best New Poets 2014,* and *The Breakbeat Poets,* among others.

Jody Rambo holds an MFA in poetry from Colorado State University. She is the author of the chapbook *Tethering World* (Kent State University Press, 2011). Her poems have appeared in *Gulf Coast, The Journal, Quarterly West, Sycamore Review, Salamander, The Virginia Quarterly Review,* among others. She is the recipient of Individual Excellence Awards from the Ohio Arts Council, the 2015 Wabash Prize for Poetry, and the 2015 Janet McCabe Poetry Prize. She lives in Springfield, Ohio.

Cintia Santana's work has appeared in *Beloit Poetry Journal, Michigan Quarterly Review, The Missouri Review, Pleiades, RHINO, Spillway, The Threepenny Review,* and other journals. She teaches poetry and fiction workshops in Spanish, as well as literary translation courses, at Stanford University. Santana is the recipient of fellowships from CantoMundo and the Djerassi Resident Artist Program.

Caitlin Scarano holds an MA from Bowling Green State University and an MFA from the University of Alaska Fairbanks. She was the winner of the 2015 Indiana Review Poetry Prize, judged by Eduardo Corral. She has two poetry chapbooks: *The White Dog Year* (dancing girl press, 2015) and *The Salt and Shadow Coiled* (Zoo Cake Press, 2015). Her debut collection of poems will be released in fall 2017 by Write Bloody Publishing. She is currently a PhD candidate in poetry at the University of Wisconsin–Milwaukee.

GAETAN SGRO is a writer and a physician who went into medicine for the stories. His poems have appeared in *The Bellevue Literary Review, Blueline, The Healing Muse, JAMA,* and other fine publications. He lives with his wife and two daughters in a row house with sea-green trim, and blogs at www.wardstories.org.

CHARIF SHANAHAN is the author of *Into Each Room We Enter without Knowing* (SIU Press, 2017), winner of the 2015 Crab Orchard Series in Poetry First Book Award. His poems have appeared in *Baffler, Boston Review, Callaloo, Literary Hub, New Republic, Poetry International, Prairie Schooner,* and elsewhere. A Cave Canem graduate fellow, he has received awards and fellowships from the Academy of American Poets, the Frost Place, the Fulbright Program, and the Millay Colony for the Arts. Currently, he is a Stegner Fellow in Poetry at Stanford University.

JEN SIRAGANIAN is a Bay Area poet and author of the chapbook *Fracture.* A Pushcart Prize nominee, she is the recipient of scholarships from the Community of Writers at Squaw Valley and Napa Valley Writers' Conference. Her poems have appeared in journals such as *cream city review, Mid-American Review, Smartish Pace, Barrow Street, Southwest Review, Natural Bridge, Catamaran Literary Reader,* and *The Squaw Valley Review,* and the anthologies *Nothing But the Truth So Help Me God* and *Not Somewhere Else But Here: A Contemporary Anthology of Women and Place.* Her website is www.jensiraganian.com.

Born in Sri Lanka, PIREENI SUNDARALINGAM is co-editor of *Indivisible: An Anthology of Contemporary South Asian American Poetry* (U. Arkansas Press, 2010), winner of the 2011 Northern California Book Award & PEN Josephine Miles Award. Her poetry has been published in literary journals such as *The American Poetry Review, Ploughshares,* and *Prairie Schooner,* as well as anthologies including Amnesty's *101 Poems for Human Rights,* and translated into five languages. Literary awards include a San Francisco Arts Commission award, the PEN Rosenthal Fellowship, and fellowships from Djerassi & the Berlin Academy of Art. Based in San Francisco, she is currently completing a poetry manuscript exploring her memories of the Sri Lankan civil war.

TALIN TAHAJIAN grew up near Boston. Her poetry has appeared in *Kenyon Review Online, Indiana Review, Passages North, Best New Poets 2014*, and *Columbia Poetry Review*. She has a chapbook, *The smallest thing on Earth* (Bloom Books, 2017), and edits poetry for the *Adroit Journal*. She's currently a student at the University of Cambridge, where she studies English literature.

PETER TWAL is an electrical engineer living in Lafayette, Indianna. His works have appeared in *Kenyon Review Online, Ninth Letter Online, Third Coast, Berkeley Poetry Review, Crab Creek Review, Tinderbox Poetry Journal, Public Pwool, Quarterly West, cream city review, The Journal, Devil's Lake, RHINO, Booth, Yemassee, New Delta Review, Forklift, Ohio, DIAGRAM, Bat City Review, New Orleans Review*, and elsewhere. Peter is a recipient of the Samuel and Mary Anne Hazo Poetry Award and earned his MFA from the University of Notre Dame. You can find more of his work at www.petertwal.com.

MATTHEW WIMBERLEY grew up in the Blue Ridge Mountains. His chapbook *Snake Mountain Almanac* was selected by Eduardo C. Corral and Ron Mohring as the winner of the 2014 Rane Arroyo Chapbook Contest from Seven Kitchens Press. Winner of the 2015 William Matthews Prize from the Asheville Poetry Review, and a finalist for the 2015 Narrative Poetry Contest, his writing has appeared in *The Greensboro Review, The Missouri Review, Narrative, Orion, The Paris-American, Poet Lore, Rattle, Shenandoah, Verse Daily*, and others. Wimberley received his MFA from New York University where he worked with children at St. Mary's Hospital as a Starworks Fellow. Wimberley was a finalist for the 2016 Crab Orchard Series in Poetry First Book Award.

KARL ZUEHLKE's poetry has appeared in *The Loaded Bicycle, DIAGRAM, Jazz Cigarette, Inscape: A Journal of Literature and Art,* and elsewhere. He won Best Creative Presentation at the University of North Texas's Critical Voices Conference 2014 for translations of an East German Poet. A former Lannan Fellow and interviews editor for *The American Literary Review*, he lives in Denton, Texas, completing his PhD.

Participating Writing Programs

American University
american.edu/cas/literature/mfa

Auburn University
cla.auburn.edu/english/graduate-
    studies/ma/concentration-in-
    creative-writing

Fine Arts Work Center
fawc.org

**Florida International University's
MFA Program**
english.fiu.edu/creative-writing

**Florida State University
MFA Program**
english.fsu.edu/crw

**Jackson Center for Creative
Writing at Hollins University**
hollinsmfa.wordpress.com

**University of Illinois at Chicago
Program for Writers**
engl.uic.edu/cw

Kansas State University
k-state.edu/english/programs/cw

**McNeese State University
MFA Program**
mfa.mcneese.edu

**Minnesota State University
Mankato**
english.mnsu.edu/cw

Monmouth University
monmouth.edu/school-of-human-
    ities-social-sciences/ma-english.
    aspx

**New Mexico Highlands
University**
nmhu.edu/current-students/
    graduate/arts-and-sciences/
    english

**New Mexico State University
MFA Program**
english.nmsu.edu/
    graduate-programs/mfa

New School Writing Program
newschool.edu/writing

North Carolina State
MFA Program
english.chass.ncsu.edu/graduate/
mfa

Northwestern School of
Professional Studies
sps.northwestern.edu/
program-areas/graduate/
creative-writing

Ohio University Creative Writing
ohio.edu/cas/english/grad/
creative-writing

The Ohio State University
MFA Program
english.osu.edu/mfa

Pacific University
Master of Fine Arts in Writing
pacificu.edu/as/mfa

San Diego State University
mfa.sdsu.edu

Sarah Lawrence College
MFA in Writing
sarahlawrence.edu/writing-mfa

Southeast Missouri State
University
semo.edu/english

Stony Brook Southampton
stonybrook.edu/southampton/mfa/
cwl

Texas Tech University Creative
Writing Program
depts.ttu.edu/english/cw

University of British Columbia
Creative Writing Program
creativewriting.ubc.ca

University of Connecticut
Graduate School
creativewriting.uconn.edu

University of Idaho MFA
uidaho.edu/class/english/graduate/
mfa-creative-writing

University of Iowa
Writers' Workshop
writersworkshop.uiowa.edu

University of Kansas
englishcw.ku.edu

Univeristy of Massachusetts Boston
MFA Program in Creative Writing
umb.edu/academics/cla/english/
grad/mfa

University of Massachusetts
MFA for Poets and Writers
umass.edu/englishmfa

University of Memphis MFA
memphis.edu/english/graduate/
    mfa/creative_writing.php

University of Missouri
english.missouri.edu/creative-
    writing.html

University of North Texas
english.unt.edu/creative-writing-0

University of Notre Dame
Creative Writing Program
english.nd.edu/creative-writing

University of South Carolina
artsandsciences.sc.edu/engl/
    mfa-program-carolina

University of South Florida
english.usf.edu/graduate/
    concentrations/cw/degrees

University of Southern
Mississippi
usm.edu/english/center-writers

University of Texas
Michener Center for Writers
utexas.edu/academic/mcw

University of Utah
english.utah.edu

Vermont College of Fine Arts
MFA in Writing
vcfa.edu

Virginia Tech
MFA in Creative Writing
http://liberalarts.vt.edu/academics/
    graduate-programs.html

Western Michigan University
wmich.edu/english

West Virginia University
creativewriting.wvu.edu

Participating Magazines

32 Poems
32poems.com

AGNI Magazine
bu.edu/agni

Alligator Juniper
alligatorjuniper.org

Apple Valley Review
applevalleyreview.com

apt
apt.aforementionedproductions
.com

Arsenic Lobster Poetry Journal
arseniclobster.magere.com

ARTS & LETTERS
artsandletters.gcsu.edu

Beloit Poetry Journal
bpj.org

Birmingham Poetry Review
uab.edu/cas/englishpublications/
birmingham-poetry-review

Booth: A Journal
booth.butler.edu

Boxcar Poetry Review
boxcarpoetry.com

cahoodaloodaling
cahoodaloodaling.com

Carve Magazine
carvezine.com

Copper Nickel
copper-nickel.org

Crazyhorse
crazyhorse.cofc.edu

Cumberland River Review
crr.trevecca.edu

Ecotone
ecotonemagazine.org

EVENT Magazine
eventmagazine.ca

Fjords Review
fjordsreview.com

Free State Review
freestatereview.com

Gingerbread House
gingerbreadhouselitmag.com

Grist: The Journal for Writers
gristjournal.com

Guernica
guernicamag.com

Hamilton Arts & Letters
HALmagazine.com

Hardly Doughnuts
hardlydoughnuts.com

Harvard Review
harvardreview.org

Hermeneutic Chaos Literary Journal
hermeneuticchaosjournal.com

Image
imagejournal.org

inter|rupture
interrupture.com

IthacaLit
ithacalit.com

Juked
juked.com

Lunch Ticket
lunchticket.org

Melancholy Hyperbole
melancholyhyperbole.com

*Memorious: A Journal of New Verse
& Fiction*
memorious.org

Muzzle Magazine
muzzlemagazine.com

Naugatuck River Review
naugatuckriverreview.com

New England Review
nereview.com

Nimrod International Journal
utulsa.edu/nimrod

One Throne Magazine
onethrone.com

Ploughshares
pshares.org

Poetry
poetrymagazine.org

Poets on Growth
poetsongrowth.tumblr.com

Pretty Owl Poetry
prettyowlpoetry.com

Quarterly West
quarterlywest.com

Raleigh Review
RaleighReview.org

Rat's Ass Review
ratsassreview.net

Red Paint Hill Poetry Journal
redpainthill.com

Room Magazine
roommagazine.com

Ruminate Magazine
ruminatemagazine.com

Southern Indiana Review
usi.edu/sir

Southwest Review
smu.edu/southwestreview

Spillway
spillway.org

storySouth
storysouth.com

Sugar House Review
SugarHouseReview.com

Sycamore Review
sycamorereview.com

Tahoma Literary Review
tahomaliteraryreview.com

The Account
theaccountmagazine.com

The Adroit Journal
theadroitjournal.org

The Believer
believermag.com

The Bitter Oleander
bitteroleander.com

The Boiler Journal
theboilerjournal.com

The Cossack Review
thecossackreview.com

The Georgia Review
thegeorgiareview.com

The Journal
english.osu.edu/mfa

The Lascaux Review
lascauxreview.com

The Los Angeles Review
losangelesreview.org

The MacGuffin
schoolcraft.edu/macguffin

The Pinch
pinchjournal.com

The Poet's Billow
thepoetsbillow.org

The Southeast Review
southeastreview.org

The Southern Review
thesouthernreview.org

Thrush Poetry Journal
thrushpoetryjournal.com

Tinderbox Poetry Journal
tinderboxpoetry.com

Up the Staircase Quarterly
upthestaircase.org

Virginia Quarterly Review
vqronline.org

Water-Stone Review
waterstonereview.com

Willow Springs
willowspringsmagazine.org

MARY SZYBIST is most recently the author of *Incarnadine*, winner of the 2013 National Book Award for Poetry. She is the recipient of fellowships from the Guggenheim Foundation, the National Endowment for the Arts, the Rona Jaffe Foundation, the Library of Congress, the Rockefeller Foundation's Bellagio Center, and the Lannan Foundation. Her first book, *Granted*, won the 2004 GLCA New Writers Award and was a finalist for the National Book Critics Circle Award. She has taught at the University of Iowa Writers' Workshop, the University of California at Berkeley, and the MFA Program for Writers at Warren Wilson College. She now lives in Portland, Oregon, where she teaches at Lewis & Clark College.

JEB LIVINGOOD is a lecturer at the University of Virginia, associate director of the UVA Creative Writing Program, and faculty advisor for *Meridian*.